I am
I CAN
I WILL

A Guided Journal of Self-Discovery
for Black Girls, with Inspiring
Role Models, Quotes, and Affirmations

Dr. Cynthia Jacobs Carter & Ruth Chamblee
Illustrations by Steffi Walthall

workman
New York

NAME: _____

This book honors my ancestors and family members, first and foremost, my mother and cousin-sisters, Flossie Jacobs Purnell, Constance Downing, and Pam Baker, respectively. I honor my father, Charles Purnell, and certainly my husband, Karl, who inspires and supports me always. I celebrate my daughter, Ahyoka, sons, and grandchildren—especially for this book—my six granddaughters, Zoë, Umm Kulthum, Fatima Zahra, Chayel, Maya Haley, and Ahyah Arielle, who are already changing the world for the better with their amazing words and actions. The golden threads that bind us are never broken. — *Cynthia*

I offer my humblest gratitude to the multitude of women throughout time and across the African Diaspora who share their ancestral wisdom with us and whose powerful voices have spoken through our writing. This book would not have been possible without the love and support of my husband, Trevor Lee, and my children, Cameron and Justin Lee, who also lent me their opinions, advice, and research skills. Finally, I thank you, who holds this book in your hands. You honor our foremothers with your presence, and you add your uniqueness to the story we all share. — *Ruth*

ISBN 978-1-5235-1457-1

Design by Lourdes Ubidia
Cover illustration by Steffi Walthall

Workman books are available at special discounts when purchased in bulk for premiums and sales promotions as well as for fundraising or educational use. Special editions or book excerpts can also be created to specification. For details, please contact special.markets@hbgusa.com.

Workman Publishing Co., Inc., a subsidiary of Hachette Book Group, Inc.
1290 Avenue of the Americas
New York, NY 10104

workman.com

WORKMAN is a registered trademark of Workman Publishing Co., Inc., a subsidiary of Hachette Book Group, Inc.

Printed in China on responsibly sourced paper.

First printing December 2023

10 9 8 7 6 5 4 3 2 1

ARE YOU READY?

You're about to go on a serious trip. By serious we mean amazing and awesome, exciting and eye-opening, creative and cool. And the trip? Well, it's a journey of self-discovery, and it's all about you.

What are *your* thoughts, ideas, imaginings? What are *your* special talents, and how can you enhance them and develop others? What are *your* challenges, and what will you do to overcome them? This journal is *your* journey. Only you can fill in the blanks. I am _____! I can _____! I will _____! Don't let anyone define you, but you.

But wait. A serious trip calls for serious traveling companions. Did you think you would have to go it alone? Not a chance. You will be joined by incredible women, from queens of ancient Africa to superstar scientists, creators, athletes, and leaders of today. Each of these women is a complex person with many life experiences, points of view, challenges, and strengths. We have chosen to highlight a single idea or moment in their lives so that you can explore what it means to you. If particular women "speak" to you strongly, we encourage you to read more about them, as each is an icon in her own right and has much of great value to say. Most importantly, we want you to realize that you descend from this long line of extraordinary Black women who at times in their lives asked themselves "Who am I and what is my place in the world?" They have journeyed this path before you and can guide you as you search for answers to the same questions and define the who and what for yourself.

By reading each woman's own words and getting a brief glimpse into her life, you will explore the concepts of resilience, creativity, leadership, and other empowering qualities. A series of questions and suggestions will encourage you to reflect on these qualities in your own life, both as it is now and in your vision for how it can be. Go ahead and make this journal your own creation and a reflection of you! Write random thoughts, pose questions to yourself, craft poems or stories to express your feelings. Draw pictures and doodles. Make plans and see them through. There are no limits on how you choose to transform the blank spaces.

Now, before beginning a journey, it's always wise to have a map. Even if you don't know your final destination—and that's the fun of exploration—you should have some markers to help you get from here to there. In this journal, you'll find three "signposts" that are meant to guide you in discovering who you are, what you're capable of, and what you'll do in the amazing journey of your life.

- **SIGNPOST #1: I** *am*—In this section, think about what unique qualities, beliefs, knowledge, and experiences make you YOU.

- **SIGNPOST #2: I** CAN—In this section, think about what challenges you will take on and what you expect from the world.

- **SIGNPOST #3: I** *WILL*—In this section, think about what dreams, goals, and promises you will fulfill for yourself and for others.

If you are feeling a certain way and want to skip to another signpost in the book, go right ahead. This is your journey and you chart the path. Go straight through, or skip around and circle back, as long as you keep moving. By the time you finish, you will have created a beautiful expression of your thoughts, feelings, fears, triumphs, and dreams that is as unique and special as you!

— *Ruth and Cynthia*

P.S. We grew up being taught by our mothers that young people never address adults by their first names. It just wasn't considered respectful. We always added "Miss" to their first name if we wanted to be friendlier and less formal. In this book, we want you to feel very comfortable with your guides, so we're using their first names. Rest assured, we have MAJOR respect for all of them and we know you will, too. We don't think they'll mind. But if you ever happen to encounter any of these women in person, do what our mommas taught us!

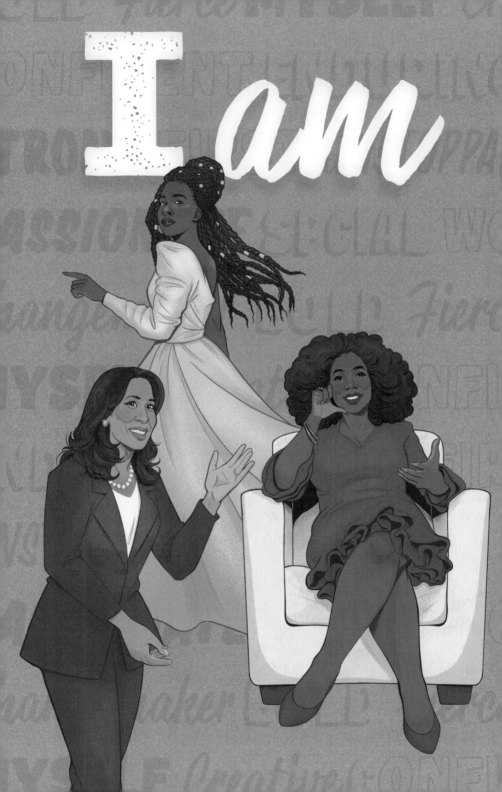

LOÏS MAILOU JONES (1905–1998)
I AM WHAT I CREATE.
I AM
not
ANONYMOUS

> ## "THE WONDERFUL THING ABOUT BEING AN ARTIST IS THAT THERE IS NO END TO CREATIVE EXPRESSION. PAINTING IS MY LIFE; MY LIFE IS PAINTING."
> ## —LOÏS MAILOU JONES

The energy and colors of Africa, France, and the Caribbean burst from the works of Loïs Mailou Jones, a prominent painter of the 1920s and '30s Black artistic movement known as the Harlem Renaissance. Loïs loved these places not only because African Americans were embraced and respected there, but because the landscapes and cultures filled her with excitement and inspiration. Her bold and abstract designs reflected the colorful kente cloth of African royalty and the lush green mountains of Haiti. Her images of expressive masks and religious symbols strengthened her spiritual connections. Most of all, Loïs loved painting the women, who were revered as wise leaders in their societies. They worked, prayed, sang, and danced across her canvases, feeding her own energy. As her creative spirit grew, so did her confidence. Loïs's paintings were sought after in Paris, but in the United States her works were often rejected by galleries and museums because she was Black. Loïs did not give up. She was determined to show that Black artists were talented by bringing the colors, textures, and shapes of Congo's vibrant costumes, France's rugged Pyrenees, and the Caribbean's bustling markets to the most famous American museums. She began submitting her paintings under the name "Anonymous." Soon they graced the walls of the nation's most renowned museums, where they hang today—now above her own name.

I am I CAN I WILL

What subject or activity do you love so much that you could "become" it?

Draw a picture based on a person or a place that inspires you.

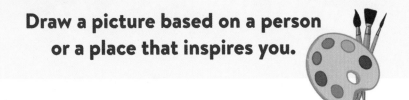

> ## "I WAS THE CONDUCTOR OF THE UNDERGROUND RAILROAD FOR EIGHT YEARS, AND I CAN SAY WHAT MOST CONDUCTORS CAN'T SAY: I NEVER RAN MY TRAIN OFF THE TRACK, AND I NEVER LOST A PASSENGER."
> ## —HARRIET TUBMAN

Harriet Tubman refused to accept failure. After escaping nearly thirty years of slavery in Maryland, she dedicated her life to freeing others from slavery and from unjust laws that kept Black people from voting. She became known as "Moses" because, like the biblical hero, she led her people out of captivity, traveling treacherous routes by night and hiding or wearing clever disguises during the day. Harriet knew how to find the safe houses with secret hideaways, the boatmen offering passage across rivers, and the countless sympathetic helpers that were all part of the Underground Railroad. If frightened runaways failed to follow her strict rules or tried to turn back, risking death or capture for everyone, she issued fierce warnings and even flashed her pistol. During the Civil War, her knowledge of the land made her an invaluable scout and spy for the Union Army. With absolute confidence and shrewd leadership, she became the first woman to command a major US military operation when, in 1863, she led one hundred and fifty Black soldiers to rescue seven hundred enslaved people in South Carolina. After the war, Harriet continued fighting for freedom and equality, raising her powerful voice in support of all women's right to vote. Though she endured many challenges in life, Harriet Tubman never prayed for an easy way out, but only for "God to make me strong and able to fight."

What qualities do you think are important for a good leader to have? Why?

Is there someone in your life who always stands up for what is right and fair? How can you learn from their example?

How might you show leadership in your life?
(Some examples are joining the school council
or initiating a club activity.)

AMANDA GORMAN (B. 1998)

I AM A VOICE FOR MY PEOPLE, MY GENERATION, MYSELF.

"WE ARE THE NEW GENERATION—AND YOU'D BETTER WATCH OUT." —AMANDA GORMAN

Amanda Gorman stepped up to the podium at the US Capitol during the January 20, 2021, inauguration of President Joseph R. Biden. With grace and confidence, the nation's first Youth Poet Laureate recited the poem she had penned for the occasion: "The Hill We Climb." Giving voice to everyone who has struggled, she was reciting her own story and expressing her own dreams, while captivating the whole world. Raised with her twin sister by a single mother, Amanda was challenged by hearing and speech disorders that made it difficult for her to hear, process, and pronounce certain letters. But she found joy in reading and writing and soon was using them to overcome her challenges. She loved to sing, and that helped, too. When First Lady–elect Jill Biden first heard Amanda recite, she was so impressed that she recommended the talented young woman to be the inaugural poet. As Amanda approached the podium on that cold January day to deliver her message of healing and hope, few would know that she used to sing the hit *Hamilton* song "Aaron Burr, Sir" every day to teach herself to pronounce the letter "r" correctly. The words of this young Black woman touched millions. An activist on race, feminism, marginalization, and oppression, Amanda is also a fashionista who believes that her identity as a poet is made stronger by the visual aesthetic of her clothes. She shines in bold reds and yellows. And the phrase on her favorite T-shirt, "Wakanda Forever," speaks boldly of her pride for her community.

Write a poem or statement about your life so far. Give it a meaningful title.

What meaningful message can you share with others—whether from your front porch at home or on a world stage?

Amanda's poem "The Hill We Climb" helps us think about where we've come as a country, and where we're headed. What would your hill look like? Draw it below—including what you've overcome, and where you want to go.

QUEEN HATSHEPSUT
(CA. 1500—1458 BCE)

I AM CONFIDENT AND ENDURING.

"MY COMMAND STANDS FIRM LIKE THE MOUNTAINS."
—QUEEN HATSHEPSUT

One of only three known female pharaohs in ancient Egypt, Hatshepsut was born to rule. A diplomat in the ancient world, she reigned over peaceful times. Her massive trade expeditions built Egypt's wealth, as her ships overflowing with papyrus, linen, copper, and lapis lazuli made their way to the Land of Punt (where Somalia is today), then returned with ivory, ebony, gold, leopard skins, and frankincense trees. The grand temples she constructed—including Deir el-Bahri, an architectural wonder of the ancient world—left a legacy few could match. None of this came easily to a woman who lived more than three thousand years ago. Women weren't supposed to be pharaohs. But Hatshepsut was different. As if aware of her destiny, she quietly observed the successful rule of her father, Thutmose I. She then played a major role in the rule of her frail husband, Thutmose II. When his early death left an infant Thutmose III too young to rule Egypt, Hatshepsut claimed her responsibility. To protect her child, her people, and the future of Egypt, she stepped up to become a full-fledged pharaoh—someone the people believed could talk to the gods and rule with power. Instead of the graceful robes and crown of a queen, she took on the heavy headdress and false gold beard of a male ruler. She called herself Maatkare, based on the word maat—the ancient Egyptian expression for order and justice established by the gods. For ten years she cultivated maat as she mentored the young pharaoh, spread peace and prosperity, built enduring monuments, and crafted a legacy to match her unique signature: "His Majesty, Herself."

I am I CAN I WILL

What do you do, or what could you do, that makes you feel proud and confident?

Stepping up to take responsibility might be intimidating, especially if you are Black and female in an environment that is largely white and male-dominated. How can you overcome fear and hesitation and be successful?

"STAGECOACH" MARY FIELDS (CA. 1832–1914)

I AM BRAVE AND UNSTOPPABLE.

"MARY BUILT A REPUTATION OF BEING FEARLESS." —SMITHSONIAN'S NATIONAL POSTAL MUSEUM ON MARY FIELDS

In 1895, Mary Fields stepped aboard the postal stagecoach, filled with pride and determination, as the first Black woman to carry the US mail. Running the US Postal Service's remote star route, "Stagecoach Mary," as she soon was called, would bring mail to isolated pioneers in the West, connecting lonely friends and families. Freed from slavery in 1863, Mary had loaded river barges before working as a groundskeeper at a convent school in Ohio. She took great pride in her gardens, and in a gruff, commanding voice, she would stop convent residents from walking across her carefully mown lawns. When a new opportunity in Montana called, Mary moved west. She immediately embraced the rough-and-ready lifestyle. Standing six feet tall and willing to speak her mind, Mary commanded respect as a skilled builder and foreman in the town of Cascade. She was also a sharpshooter, a talent that would come in handy. With a revolver under her apron, her dog and a rifle at her side, Mary was soon maneuvering a mail-packed stagecoach across the Montana wilderness, protecting her cargo from bandits, wild animals, and harsh weather. Like anyone, she must have been fearful sometimes. But people depended on her—and she never missed a day of work. Retiring as a Montana hero, Mary was so beloved in Cascade that the schools closed each year to celebrate her birthday. Today, part of Highway 15 along her old route bears her name. So does the asteroid astronomers call "Maryfields," a fitting tribute to the trailblazing star route driver.

Is there a fearless person you admire? How do their actions inspire you?

Are there times when feeling fear is useful?
How do you know when to listen to your fears
and when to push past them?

JULIEANNA RICHARDSON (B. 1954)

I AM PASSIONATE ABOUT MY PURPOSE!

"I'M A PERSON WHO NEEDS TO LIVE A LIFE FULL OF PASSION. I WAS MOTIVATED BY MAKING A DIFFERENCE AND LEAVING A LEGACY." —JULIEANNA RICHARDSON

In the small, mostly white Ohio town where Julieanna Richardson grew up, she didn't hear many stories about Black people. In fact, as a young girl, she didn't even realize that Black people *have* our own history. During a winding path of career changes and self-discovery, Julieanna became fully immersed in the story of Black America, and she wanted to share it. She founded The HistoryMakers, now the world's largest collection of African American oral histories. The database is housed in the Library of Congress and has more than three thousand video interviews with Black artists, activists, athletes, educators, business leaders, scientists, politicians, and more. Julieanna's own life story would make a fascinating entry. Before finding her passion, she was an actress, Harvard-trained lawyer, cable administrator, and home-shopping network founder. Although she was successful in all of these fields, she realized she was following other people's dreams for her and not her own dreams for herself. She thought about a long-ago college assignment: to interview older Black people about their experiences. She discovered the richness of Black oral history and the need to preserve and share our voices, in the Black tradition going all the way back to the griots, or storytellers, of West Africa. Now, a more experienced Julieanna is recording stories again—this time for all the world to hear and celebrate. By listening to the voices of our ancestors, and to herself, Julieanna Richardson found her passion, her purpose, and her own voice.

Discovering your passion begins
with understanding yourself.
What interests you? What are your favorite
subjects? What activities do you enjoy?
What are you curious about?

Who are the griots in your life? Don't just imagine what fascinating stories they have to tell; sit down with them and ask.

With a parent's or guardian's permission, visit The HistoryMakers website at thehistorymakers.org to read about different people and their stories. What story "speaks" to you? What story of your own are you inspired to tell?

> "WHATEVER YOUR REASON FOR HOLDING ON TO RESENTMENTS, I KNOW THIS FOR SURE: THERE IS NONE WORTH THE PRICE YOU PAY IN LOST TIME."
> —OPRAH WINFREY

Oprah Winfrey is one of the most well-known, most frequently quoted, most influential women on Earth. But her success did not come easily. Born to a single mother who was just eighteen years old, Oprah's early years were spent shuttling between her grandmother, mother, and father. She felt like no one wanted her. Her mother seemed to prefer her lighter-skinned stepsister, and when Oprah performed well in school, it didn't seem to matter. Adding to this emotional pain, Oprah became the victim of repeated abuse by a male cousin, her uncle, and a family friend. In a dark place with seemingly no way out, she grew rebellious and self-destructive. Finally, at the age of fourteen, she was sent back to live with her father, a church deacon. It was a move that quite possibly saved her life. Her father became a wise mentor, providing stability, discipline, high educational standards, and a belief in a higher power, which she later called the greatest discovery of her life. Oprah could have allowed bitterness and resentment to define her and her future. Instead, she focused on healing from the pain of her childhood and creating a positive, successful life for herself. No matter how high her star rises or how important her voice becomes, Oprah remains down-to-earth, compassionate, and dedicated to sharing her hard-earned wisdom.

How can you shake yourself out of a bad mood or keep negative feelings away? Write down five happy, fun things that you like to do and do one whenever you need a boost of positivity.

_____

_____

_____

_____

_____

_____

Holding on to disagreements, resentments, and other negative emotions is like having angry, prickly critters banging around inside you. They can make you sick, and they're a waste of precious time. Let's get rid of them! Find a blank piece of paper and cut it into five strips. Write one resentment, or negative emotion, on each strip. One by one, read it, fold it, and put it in an envelope. Then, close your eyes and say aloud, "Go away!" When you finish, seal the envelope full of negativity and throw it in the trash.

Sometimes people with more life experience can suggest a different way to think about things. The next time you have a problem or difficult decision to make, which of your elders might you ask for advice? What will you ask?

"GIRLS AND WOMEN OF OUR RACE MUST NOT BE AFRAID TO TAKE HOLD OF BUSINESS ENDEAVOR AND, BY PATIENT INDUSTRY, CLOSE ECONOMY, DETERMINED EFFORT, AND CLOSE APPLICATION TO BUSINESS, WRING [OUT] SUCCESS."
—MADAM C. J. WALKER

America's first Black woman self-made millionaire, Madam C. J. Walker began "making" herself at an early age. She was born as Sarah Breedlove to formerly enslaved parents and had little education. By the time she was orphaned at the age of seven, she had already grown accustomed to hard labor in the cotton fields of Louisiana. Her story could have ended there, but she was determined to escape that fate. After marrying, having a child, and becoming a widow by age twenty, she took her daughter to St. Louis in search of a better life. She worked from dawn to dusk as a laundress. Perhaps due to stress or harsh styling techniques, her hair began to thin. After trying many hair products with no success, she began to make her own. When she saw that her hair grew back thick and healthy, she also saw something else—a business opportunity to sell her unique product. First sold by word-of-mouth and door-to-door, Sarah's hair tonic became a must-have for every Black woman. Soon, she was developing new marketing techniques to spread her product across the nation, then around the world. She created an empire and shared her success by hiring twenty thousand Black women into her prestigious company. When Sarah remarried, she called her business after herself—the Madam C. J. Walker Manufacturing Company—which quickly became a household name.

Whether you want to be a businesswoman, an artist, or the lead in the school play, confidence and courage are keys to success. You are your biggest champion! Write down some encouraging statements that you can repeat to yourself as you reach for your goals.

I'VE GOT THIS!

Think like a businesswoman and come up with some ideas for a new club at school, a class event, or a fundraiser. What talents or skills do you have that might help it succeed? Sketch out a plan. Then make it happen step by step— enjoy the journey!

KAMALA DEVI HARRIS (B. 1964)

I AM THE FIRST, BUT NOT THE LAST.

"SURROUND YOURSELF WITH REALLY GOOD FRIENDS. HAVE PEOPLE AROUND YOU WHO CHEER YOU ON, AND APPLAUD YOU, AND SUPPORT YOU, AND ARE HONEST WITH YOU." —KAMALA HARRIS

The first Black, first South Asian, and first woman to become vice president of the United States, Kamala Devi Harris is a leader for the twenty-first century. Elected in 2020, she is a fearless advocate for healthcare reform, immigrant family rights, the LGBTQIA+ community, and other issues. She also believes in the power of female connections—especially women opening doors for other women, then helping them through. Born to an Indian mother and a Jamaican father, both immigrants, she was raised mostly by her mother, a scientist who expected excellence. Kamala began kindergarten by being bussed away from her own neighborhood and friends to a white school several miles away. When she complained, her mother simply told her to *do something about it!*—and Kamala did. She found friends who shared her sharp mind, her sense of fairness, and her determination to be a confident Black woman. Learning to build her own support system inspired her to encourage other girls. When she attended the historically Black Howard University, Kamala counseled women classmates to stand up for themselves, and she studied laws to protect women, children, and immigrants. Her career as a lawyer and attorney general of California led her to the US Senate, then to the nation's second-highest office. Taking her own advice may well open that next door for Kamala Harris and the women who come after her.

Who are your biggest supporters and how do they help you?

How are you supportive, encouraging, and honest with your friends?

Write a thank-you note to someone in your life who opened a door for you.

OPPORTUNITY

MAE JEMISON (B. 1956)

I AM WHERE I BELONG.

"ONCE I GOT INTO SPACE . . . I FELT LIKE I HAD A RIGHT TO BE ANYWHERE IN THIS UNIVERSE, THAT I BELONGED HERE AS MUCH AS ANY SPECK OF STARDUST, ANY COMET, ANY PLANET." —MAE JEMISON

When Mae Jemison blasted out of Earth's orbit on the space shuttle *Endeavour*, she became the first Black woman to enter the vastness of space. But for her, it was more than the high point in a lifetime of scientific study, advanced degrees, achievements, and awards. It was a very personal moment—a sense of rightness, calm, and belonging. Mae loved science from an early age, especially astronomy. She spent hours at the library reading about it and watched many Apollo launches on TV. It bothered her that there were no female astronauts, and Mae became determined to one day travel into space. But her path to the stars was far from straight as she explored many diverse interests along the way. The difficulty of being one of only a few Black students in her class at Stanford University led Mae to get involved with the Black Student Union. After earning degrees in chemical engineering and African & African American studies, Mae went on to graduate from medical school. She continued looking for unique ways to combine her interests and talents, which included speaking four languages, and soon she was doing humanitarian and medical work in Cuba, Thailand, Kenya, and other parts of Africa. Finally, in 1985, she decided to follow her childhood dream and applied for NASA's astronaut training program. There, her diverse experiences came together to help launch her into space—where she felt connected with the whole universe.

I am I can I will

Write about or draw a situation in which you feel completely comfortable and confident. How can you take this feeling into other areas of your life?

What do you most love to read about, study, or do? How might these interests influence what you do as you get older and become an adult?

VIOLA DAVIS (B. 1965)
I AM SPECIAL AND WORTHY.

"I LOOK BACK AT PICTURES OF MYSELF, AND I'M LIKE, 'YOU WERE FABULOUS.' I WISH I WOULD HAVE KNOWN THAT THEN. I WOULD TELL MY YOUNGER SELF JUST BE YOURSELF—THAT WHO YOU ARE IS GOOD ENOUGH."
—VIOLA DAVIS

As an actor, Viola Davis's job is to stop being herself and to take on the appearance, behavior, and life of another person. To do that as well as she does, with real emotion and credibility, means drawing deeply on her own life experiences. It also means looking at herself honestly and understanding who she is before she can *become* someone else. Viola is one of the most talented and honored actors of her generation, winning countless awards, including the first Emmy ever won by a Black woman for a leading dramatic role on prime-time television and a complete EGOT. But she remembers being the little six-year-old, dark-skinned girl who grew up desperately poor and subjected to the isolation and racism of a small, mostly white town. She was cursed at, called names, and insulted so much that she began to believe she wasn't pretty or worthy of better treatment. But everything changed when she saw Cicely Tyson in the film *The Autobiography of Miss Jane Pittman*. Watching Cicely on screen, Viola decided that if a dark-skinned person with full lips could be an actor, then this would be her path. While she went on to become highly respected on stage, television, and film, she also learned to accept and embrace the difficulties and failures in her life. She inspires young girls who feel like she did growing up to ignore the haters, believe in themselves, and know that their future can be bright.

Write down at least five positive, supportive, and loving statements about yourself.

Write a letter to your future self, maybe at age twenty-one or older. What do you want that person to know about you at this age?

SHIRLEY CHISHOLM
(1924–2005)

I AM A
CHANGE MAKER.

"DON'T LISTEN TO THOSE WHO SAY <u>YOU CAN'T</u>. LISTEN TO THE VOICE INSIDE YOURSELF THAT SAYS, <u>I CAN</u>." —SHIRLEY CHISHOLM

On Inauguration Day 2021, Shirley Chisholm's presence was felt. She was reflected in Vice President Kamala Harris's purple suit, a nod to Shirley's favorite color. Congresswoman Barbara Lee honored Shirley by wearing the pearls Shirley had once worn. The first Black congresswoman's can-do spirit inspires Black women to this day. Born Shirley Anita St. Hill to a New York factory laborer from Guyana and a seamstress from Barbados, she grew up in a home where everyone read and discussed the news. This made the bright young girl determined to change the injustices she saw in her Bedford-Stuyvesant neighborhood—crumbling housing, poor schools, few jobs, rising crime. It also made her a fearless debater, who looked like a giant to her opponents as she called out problems, debated solutions, and became a force for change. She saw the future she wanted for herself and others—and she went for it. Working as a teacher, then a local politician, she helped her community flourish. In 1968, she took a running leap for US Congress, which was filled with white men resistant to change. But "Fighting Shirley," as she was known, won. She never gave up working for all people throughout her fifteen years in Congress. Even when she broke new ground as the first Black female candidate for president of the United States, she was most proud to listen to people from all walks of life and to help them find better jobs, education, and homes—to be a politician for the people.

I am I CAN I WILL

What causes or issues make you want to stand up and work for change?

Name the trailblazers
who inspire you the most.

CHANGE IS NOW!

I am I CAN I WILL

Take a moment to think about the women you've met, and write what you've learned about yourself on this journey so far. Fill in the spaces below when you're ready. You can come back to this page to review your statements or to fill them in at any time.

Declarations for Myself

I AM:

I AM:

I AM:

I AM:

I AM:

"MY DOCTORS TOLD ME I WOULD NEVER WALK AGAIN. MY MOTHER TOLD ME I WOULD. I BELIEVED MY MOTHER." —WILMA RUDOLPH

Wilma Rudolph became a champion simply by surviving her childhood. Born weighing only four and a half pounds, she contracted polio at age four, quickly followed by pneumonia and scarlet fever. Any one of these illnesses might have killed her. Instead, they left her unable to walk without a heavy leg brace. Wilma's mother took her on a hundred-mile round-trip bus ride two times each week for medical treatments, and she did regular physical therapy at home. After five years of dedicated and difficult work, Wilma stunned her doctors when she removed her brace and walked on her own. But she didn't stop there. Soon she was the fastest runner in her elementary school and then on her high school track team. She eventually caught the attention of the Tennessee State University women's track coach who worked with her to become the youngest member of the 1956 US Olympic team. She was just sixteen. In 1960, only seven years out of her leg brace, Wilma set a record as the fastest woman runner in the world. She stood proudly on the Olympic podium as the first American woman to win three gold medals at a single Olympics. Although Wilma's greatest challenge and greatest victory were both connected to her physical body, her path to success began in her mind. Wilma Rudolph not only believed she would walk again, she believed she would run.

**Think about a challenge you face. Write
a letter to yourself that you can read any
time you need a little boost of confidence.**

What do you do when you receive discouraging news? What are some things you can do to make yourself feel better in the moment?

Imagine yourself performing at your best.
What does that look like? How do you feel?
Draw a picture as a reminder!

"I REFUSED TO TAKE NO FOR AN ANSWER."
—BESSIE COLEMAN

essie Coleman became America's first Black female pilot at a time when Black people couldn't vote, couldn't mingle with white people, and certainly couldn't attend flight school. But as a teenager, she became fascinated with the emerging field of aviation and nothing was going to stop her from spreading her wings. Although she finished eighth grade at the top of her class, there was no money to continue her education, so she moved to Chicago with her older brother. There she worked hard and boldly asked influential people for help, which set her on a path toward her goal of learning to fly. Denied training in the United States because she was Black, Bessie found a French aviation school that would accept her. She learned to speak French, moved to France, and in 1921, she became the first African American to earn a prestigious international pilot's license. Bessie especially loved doing the loops and rolls of stunt flying, and soon she returned to the United States to begin her trailblazing career. At first she was completely ignored by the mainstream press. But she convinced reporters that she was exciting, adventurous, and newsworthy. Soon her graceful and daring performances were wowing crowds who paid to see her as the barnstorming sensation "Queen Bess." She refused to perform before segregated audiences and used her status as a celebrity to encourage other young Black Americans to pursue careers as pilots. When she died at just thirty-four years old, her plan to open a flight school for Black aviators was unrealized. But Bessie Coleman's courage and perseverance live on to inspire every girl who dreams of controlling her own destiny.

Can you remember a time when
someone told you, "No, you can't,"
when you wanted to accomplish something
important to you? How did you react? What
did you or could you do to overcome the "No"?

Think of something you've done that could inspire someone else to work toward a goal. What advice would you give them?

HABEN GIRMA (B. 1988)

I CAN DO
GREAT THINGS
MY OWN WAY

"YOU HAVE THE POWER TO INFLUENCE YOUR FUTURE. KEEP LEARNING, KEEP DEVELOPING NEW WAYS TO ENGAGE WITH THE WORLD, AND KEEP BELIEVING THAT YOU HAVE TALENTS TO SHARE." —HABEN GIRMA

Haben Girma first became an advocate for herself because she was tired of eating whatever the cafeteria workers in her college dining hall chose to give her. Born deaf and blind, she couldn't see or be told what was available, and the workers didn't provide braille menus that she could read by touch. Haben was extremely independent throughout her childhood, thanks to the resources made possible by the Americans with Disabilities Act (ADA), and she was not about to give up. After she informed the cafeteria managers that they were required by the ADA to provide braille menus and that she would take legal action if they did not, they agreed. Just like that, Haben realized that the law could make a huge difference to people with disabilities and it shaped her future career path. She became the first Deafblind graduate of Harvard Law School and was her own best example of using your power to influence your future. Now she uses her personal experiences and her legal training to uphold the rights of others with disabilities and to teach the public about the benefits of being inclusive. But just like the cafeteria workers, people aren't always open to change, so she follows her own advice: If you face a challenge, it's an opportunity to come up with new solutions.

I am I CAN I WILL

Have you ever let an obstacle stand in your way of accomplishing a goal? What creative ideas can help you get past the challenges?

Write down some of the powers you have right now to influence your life and your future.

MISTY COPELAND (B. 1982)

I CAN EXCEED ALL EXPECTATIONS.

"KNOW THAT YOU CAN START LATE, LOOK DIFFERENT, BE UNCERTAIN, AND STILL SUCCEED." —MISTY COPELAND

Misty Copeland began formal dance training at thirteen, which was considered old by ballet standards. But within five years she was an award-winning dancer, performing with her dream company, the American Ballet Theatre (ABT), in New York City. Still, her success was clouded by the stress of being the only Black person among eighty dancers in the corps de ballet and the criticism that her curvy body was less than ideal for ballet. Misty wasn't what people expected a ballerina to be. But she believed in herself and kept working hard. As others began to embrace her uniqueness and her incredible talent, Misty's star quickly rose. She became ABT's first African American soloist in two decades, earning leading roles traditionally performed by white dancers, including her groundbreaking performance of Odette/Odile in *Swan Lake*. Misty was changing how people thought about ballet, creating opportunities for other dancers of color, and bringing in new audiences. Soon she made headlines again, as the first Black woman in ABT's history to be named principal dancer. Misty uses her historic achievements to support programs that increase racial and ethnic diversity in ballet. As a body image spokesperson and role model, her message to young people is to own your power and your voice, and to never let other people's words define you. Her muscular shape and brown skin made her stand out in a dance environment that loves uniformity. Now, Misty Copeland stands out because she dances in front, as a prima ballerina.

A goal is something you want to accomplish that requires you to make a plan and commit to doing the work. Give yourself at least one goal. What will you do this week—even a small step—to begin moving forward?

What are your family's expectations for you? What do your teachers and friends expect? Are these different from your own expectations?

Have you ever been labeled and judged by a stereotype such as "Black people can't do this" or "Girls can't do that"? Write down some words to describe how this made you feel. What can you do to overcome these labels and remember who *you* are?

ELIZABETH "MUMBET" FREEMAN
(CA. 1742–1829)

I CAN CONTROL
MY DESTINY.

"BY KEEPING STILL AND MINDING THINGS." —ELIZABETH "MUMBET" FREEMAN, WHEN ASKED HOW SHE LEARNED ABOUT THE LAW THAT SHE USED TO FREE HERSELF FROM SLAVERY, 1781

No one knows for certain when Elizabeth Freeman was born. In the 1700s it wasn't considered important to record the birth dates of enslaved people. She had no full name and was known only as Elizabeth, or Mumbet, for short. Like most enslaved people, she was destined to be forgotten by history. That is, until the moment she decided to change her life. How? By quietly paying attention to what she heard around her and using that information to take action. In 1776, word of the new Declaration of Independence spread across the colonies, with its message of freedom for all. Mumbet wondered if this freedom could apply to her, too. Years later, when people began discussing the newly ratified Massachusetts Constitution, Mumbet heard again that "all men are born free and equal, and have certain natural, essential, and inalienable rights." When she asked her enslaver if this meant she could be free, he claimed that these rights didn't apply to enslaved people. This made no sense to her. She turned to a young abolitionist attorney who agreed to present her case in court. Mumbet won and became the first enslaved woman in Massachusetts to win her freedom on constitutional grounds. And her lawsuit, *Brom and Bett v. Ashley*, influenced the 1783 Supreme Court ruling that ended slavery in the state. One of her first acts of freedom was to choose her own name: Elizabeth Freeman.

Some people form strong opinions about things quickly and like to speak up and take action. Others like to take a little longer to think quietly to themselves before saying how they feel or deciding what to do. Write about what feels right to you and whether it might be helpful at times to try the other way.

Do you know why your first name was chosen for you or anything about the history of your last name? What does your name mean to you? What do you want others to think when they read or hear your name?

My Name is . . .
IMPORTANT &
BRAVE

"I AM NO LONGER ACCEPTING THE THINGS I CANNOT CHANGE. I AM CHANGING THE THINGS I CANNOT ACCEPT." —ANGELA DAVIS

Angela Davis became a civil rights activist as a child attending demonstrations with her mother, and her refusal to accept injustice continues to this day. Angela grew up in a segregated area of Birmingham, Alabama. It was known as "Dynamite Hill" for the racially motivated bombings of Black homes and businesses by white supremacists in the 1950s and '60s. When she was in college, the 16th Street Baptist Church bombing, which killed four young Black girls in 1963, left her enraged and confirmed her growing belief in the need for extreme social change. Angela began studying radical political ideas, searching for ways to fight the injustices suffered by Black and oppressed people around the world. Her style of protest was aggressive, though not violent. She took on issues that made people nervous, including fighting for the rights of Black men in prison. Angela paid a price for her outspokenness. She was fired from her university teaching position and was even jailed for a crime she did not commit. With each setback, she became an even more powerful symbol of the Black struggle for social, economic, and political justice. Today, as an author, public speaker, and educator, Angela remains a passionate activist for change. Once labeled a combative figure, she is now in high demand as a visionary speaker. She was even hired to teach at the same university that had fired her for her political views. But that won't stop her from challenging them or anyone else.

Do you believe that one person really can change the world? Do you know someone, or can you think of someone, who could? How?

If you could wave a magic wand and change your school, your neighborhood, or the world for the better, what would you do? Thinking big is the first step toward acting in big, impactful ways.

Have you ever spoken up with a strong opinion or belief that is different from what your friends, family, or classmates believe? How did it feel to take a stand?

CHANGE FOR THE BETTER!

QUEEN NZINGA (CA. 1582—1663)

I CAN UNITE AND BUILD STRENGTH.

"VIRTUE IS STRONGER WHEN UNITED." —NATIONAL MOTTO OF ANGOLA AND OF EARLY RULER QUEEN NZINGA

On the lower level of the Smithsonian National Museum of African American History and Culture in Washington, DC, the life-size portrait of a regal-looking Black woman wearing a crown of gemstones is the first image visitors see. Queen Nzinga of Ndongo and Matamba (present-day Angola) was a mighty queen, revered enough to be painted for the ages. Now imagine this beautiful queen fearlessly leading an army into battle. Nzinga's story as a leader begins in 1624. For more than four decades, her people had been captured by Portuguese slave traders and sold into bondage to countries across the sea. When both Nzinga's father, the king, and her brother had died, Nzinga was left alone to rule the nation. She knew she had to unite her people against foreign invaders and bring the horrible practice of slave-trading in her country to an end. Nzinga built up her armies, bringing together communities who were once rivals, and led them to defeat the powerful Portuguese in numerous battles. At other times she cleverly negotiated with their governors to keep the peace. Nzinga succeeded in limiting the Portuguese colony to only a few square miles of her kingdom, and she dramatically reduced the enslavement of her people. With the heart of a warrior and the skills of a leader, she guided the people of her kingdom for forty years. Even when the Portuguese finally forced her from her throne, she led from afar, keeping her people united and gaining their lifelong loyalty for her courage, strength, and leadership.

Sometimes the most courageous thing
a person can do is to ask for help, especially
if they are usually confident. Do you ask for
help when you need it? Could someone help
you improve even in an area in which you excel?

How do you help and protect those
you love when they are struggling
with something difficult?

JANE BOLIN (1908–2007)

I CAN USE MY SKILLS FOR GOOD.

"FAMILIES AND CHILDREN ARE SO IMPORTANT TO OUR SOCIETY, AND TO DEDICATE YOUR LIFE TO TRYING TO IMPROVE THEIR LIVES IS COMPLETELY SATISFYING." —JANE BOLIN

When Jane Bolin learned about the horrors of lynching as a young girl, it rocked her sheltered childhood. From that point on, she became determined to contribute in her own small way to social justice. After her mother died, Jane and her three siblings were raised by a devoted single father. She spent many contented hours surrounded by the books in her father's small law office and became inspired to follow in his footsteps. She loved to read and was an excellent student, but the path was not easy. As one of the few Black students throughout her school years in the early 1900s, Jane felt ignored by her classmates and received no encouragement from her teachers. In spite of this, she graduated in the top twenty of her class at Wellesley College and became the first Black woman graduate of Yale Law School. Her lifelong concern for social justice led her to provide legal services for those who had no voice and couldn't afford to pay. Only eight years after graduating from law school, Jane was appointed the first Black woman judge in the United States and turned her full attention to serving those most in need—young people charged with crimes, mothers and children needing protection or support, and children placed for adoption. With each ruling, she ensured that children received fair treatment, guidance, and a path toward a better future. Jane Bolin's forty years as a judge improved the lives of countless people, especially children, both inside and outside her courtroom.

Have you ever been the only—or almost only—girl or Black person at an event? How did that feel and how did you handle it? What needs to be done so that someone else doesn't have to feel that way?

Complete this thought:

Children are important to society because_____.

What would you like to tell adults about how children think and feel about the world?

JOHNNETTA COLE (B. 1936)

I CAN BE, AND HELP OTHERS TO BE, ANYTHING.

> "WHAT YOU GIVE OUGHT TO BE IN DIRECT RELATIONSHIP TO WHAT YOU'VE RECEIVED. IF YOU HAVE BEEN BLESSED WITH A GREAT DEAL, THEN YOU HAVE A LOT OF GIVING TO DO." —JOHNNETTA COLE

Johnnetta Cole might say that she was "blessed" with an important discovery at the age of fifteen, during her first year at Fisk University. She realized that our heroes are real people we can learn from and follow their example. Johnnetta met one of her own heroes, the noted poet and author Arna Bontemps, and marveled that he was also an educator and held a regular job as the university librarian. Her brief but meaningful experience with this man might have inspired the young student's exploration of new directions for her life. She transferred to Oberlin College to study medicine, but an enthusiastic anthropology professor made the subject so engaging that she changed direction completely and graduated with a degree in anthropology. Her openness to exploring new opportunities continued throughout her impressive career: She became a highly respected professor of anthropology; a published author; a creator of mentorship programs for students; and the first Black woman president of Spelman College, a prestigious women's HBCU (historically Black college or university). All the time, she kept her door open to students, committed to listening and giving advice. Now she has become a hero for young people by being an active role model. Johnnetta Cole has shared so many of her life lessons with others, she must feel truly blessed.

Who are your heroes?
Why do you admire them?

Make a list of new things you'd like
to explore. Keep your favorite subjects
and after-school activities in mind, but
stay curious about how you can grow.

Have you been blessed with a lot?
What are the things, people, or aspects
of your life that make you most thankful?
Try writing a daily statement in your journal:
I am thankful for _____.

DOROTHY IRENE HEIGHT
(1912–2010)

I CAN FIGHT
FOR MY RIGHTS
AND FOR YOURS.

"GREATNESS IS NOT MEASURED BY WHAT A MAN OR WOMAN ACCOMPLISHES, BUT BY THE OPPOSITION HE OR SHE HAS OVERCOME TO REACH HIS GOALS."
—DOROTHY IRENE HEIGHT

For most of her ninety-eight years, Dorothy Irene Height modestly called herself a servant leader. But her dignified manner, powerful voice, and unwavering commitment to help all underserved communities changed the lives of millions. As a teen in the 1920s, Dorothy excelled in oratory contests, speaking out against segregation, lynching, and unequal treatment of women. Her own rights were challenged when, at the top of her class, she was accepted to New York's Barnard College then abruptly denied entry. The quota of two African Americans per year had already been met. Hurt, but fueled by the injustice, she soon entered New York University. There she laid the groundwork for her future: integrating New York's Young Women's Christian Association (YWCA) as its president; championing the rights of Black women as president of the National Council of Negro Women; and serving as the only woman among Dr. Martin Luther King Jr.'s top advisors throughout the Civil Rights Movement. Dorothy was also one of the few women invited onstage during the 1963 March on Washington. The honor was short-lived, when only the men were asked to speak. She could have been bitter, but she looked to the future, knowing there was more work to do. Dorothy advised US presidents from Eisenhower to Obama and helped pave the way for equal opportunities and equal pay for all. She may not have spoken the day MLK made his "I Have a Dream" speech, but Dorothy Height made her own dream—to open doors for others—come true.

Think about a needed change or an activity that will help people in your school or community. Why is it important to you? How can you get involved?

What obstacles have you overcome
to reach a goal? How did your
attitude help you move forward?

JANELLE MONÁE (B. 1985)

I CAN BECOME MY VISION OF MYSELF.

"I FEEL MYSELF BECOMING THE FEARLESS PERSON I HAVE DREAMT OF BEING. HAVE I ARRIVED? NO. BUT I'M CONSTANTLY EVOLVING AND CHALLENGING MYSELF TO BE UNAFRAID TO MAKE MISTAKES." —JANELLE MONÁE

Janelle Monáe Robinson wasn't always as confident as she is today. She battled fear and insecurity on her way to becoming an award-winning, Black, queer, superstar singer and actress. She grew up poor in a tough Kansas City neighborhood, but Janelle loved to sing and act in local plays. Her large, close-knit family believed in her and her dream to make it as a performer. But Janelle was afraid she couldn't live up to impossible showbiz standards. She didn't look like other Black female artists, and her cutting-edge style and sound were so different. Even so, Janelle's talent took her to the American Musical and Dramatic Academy in New York, the Atlanta music scene, and finally to superstardom, where she hid her insecurity by performing as a made-up character—Cindi Mayweather. But she knew that in order to free herself from fear, she had to open herself to others. Gradually, her song lyrics began to reveal personal aspects of her life. She began to express her interests and became a powerful voice for women's equality, especially in the music industry. Finally, she shared her most private self by coming out as queer. Janelle knows that her path of self-discovery isn't finished, but she grows stronger every day, and she wants others to do the same. Janelle Monáe's road to being a performer was also the road to becoming her truest self. And her message to young people is to never let anyone or anything stop your evolution, even if it's you.

What does becoming a fearless person mean to you? How do you become fearless?

Make a list of people you think are strong and brave. What do you have in common with them?

STEPHANIE THOMAS (B. 1970)

I CAN FIGHT FOR WHAT I DESERVE.

> # "I STYLE TO POWER AND TO EDUCATE. STYLING LETS YOU SEE THE PERSON BEFORE YOU SEE THE DISABILITY."
> ## —STEPHANIE THOMAS

When Stephanie Thomas went shopping one day, she was furious to discover more fashion options for her pet than for people with disabilities. Born missing a right thumb and toes on both feet, she was destined to face a lifetime of challenges in performing even basic tasks like buttoning a blouse. Doctors even warned her family that she would never walk independently. But Stephanie learned just like any other toddler, and eventually went so far as to become a Chicago Bulls cheerleader and pageant contestant. When someone asked why she never buttoned her left sleeve, Stephanie began researching fashion options for people with disabilities. She invented her Disability Fashion Styling System and began helping others to style themselves. She studied fashion journalism, researched clothing lines, talked to designers, and began asking disabled people what they wanted. Her goal was to convince the fashion industry to see the value in designing *for* the disabled community. Finding little interest or support, she founded her own company, Cur8able, to help empower disabled people to build confidence through clothes, makeup, and styling. Stephanie continued to speak out, finally convincing the fashion industry to feature models with disabilities. It was a start, but facing down barriers remains a lifelong crusade for Stephanie. Her reward is the satisfaction and self-esteem felt by thousands around the globe wearing clothes that reflect their style and meet their needs.

What is your own personal challenge? How can you face it with creativity and optimism?

Draw a power outfit for yourself that would make you feel confident, stylish, and able to face any obstacle that comes your way.

Take a moment to think about the women you've met, and write what you've learned about yourself on this journey so far. Fill in the spaces below when you're ready. You can come back to this page to review your statements or to fill them in at any time.

Declarations for Myself

I CAN:

I CAN:

I CAN:

I CAN:

I CAN:

MICHELLE OBAMA (B. 1964)

I WILL SHOW YOU WHO I AM AND ACCEPT WHO YOU ARE.

"THERE'S POWER IN ALLOWING YOURSELF TO BE KNOWN AND HEARD, IN OWNING YOUR UNIQUE STORY, IN USING YOUR AUTHENTIC VOICE. AND THERE'S GRACE IN BEING WILLING TO KNOW AND HEAR OTHERS."
—MICHELLE OBAMA

Michelle Obama was the first Black First Lady of the United States. But that's not the only reason she was unlike any other First Lady. She wasn't afraid to let everyone see her just being herself. She called herself "Mom-in-Chief," wore jeans and sneakers, and planted a garden on the White House lawn because she wanted kids and *everyone* to eat healthier. To encourage all Americans to get into better shape, she let us watch her sweat through all sorts of exercise, from push-ups to kickboxing to hula-hooping with hundreds of kids for her Let's Move! campaign. And when we were all struggling with the difficult events of 2020 and 2021, she admitted to feeling a little depressed, too, and let us know it was okay to ask for help. Michelle Obama is a Harvard-trained attorney, Princeton graduate, bestselling author, and fashion trendsetter. But she's also still the girl from the South Side of Chicago, and she likes to keep things real. That's why so many people of all ages find it easy to relate to her and follow her example. By letting us see her dig in the dirt, play, exercise, and struggle with problems just like we do, our accomplished and glamorous First Lady gave us the freedom to show all sides of ourselves, too.

Write several words or phrases that describe the REAL you: your personality, things you like to do, and what's important to you.

Do your friends know these things about you? If not, how would it feel for you to tell them?

On the flip side, do you know these things about your friends? How can you show them that you want to hear and know their unique stories?

ZORA NEALE HURSTON (1891–1960)

I WILL TURN BAD INTO GOOD.

"SOME PEOPLE COULD LOOK AT A MUD PUDDLE AND SEE AN OCEAN WITH SHIPS." —ZORA NEALE HURSTON

Zora Neale Hurston's teenage years could have been so different had her mother lived, but she died when Zora was only thirteen. The fifth of eight children, Zora had to contribute to the family income and help with the younger children. She dropped out of high school, worked odd jobs, and became a caregiver. Her education might have ended there, but Zora's mind was quick and curious. She began studying again while working, and at last earned her high school diploma at twenty-six years old. She raced through college and graduate school, expanding her mind through courses in literature, history, and anthropology. Zora's personal loss and intellectual gain inspired her to begin writing. Her early years of helping her family brought discipline, patience, humor, and extraordinary powers of observation. She called on these skills as she wrote several hours a day to capture the Black experience, gender issues, and racial inequality in books such as *Their Eyes Were Watching God*—today a classic. Living in New York at the dawn of the Harlem Renaissance, Zora thrived among its musicians, artists, and writers. She wove stories that captured the vibrant world around her, delving into Black folklore, portraying African-influenced music, art, and spirituality. She published books, had plays performed, and brushed shoulders with influential artists—a new life she could hardly have imagined as a young, motherless child. But Zora saw a rich, compelling story—an ocean with ships—in every mud puddle, and her writings still win her praise as the most influential Black woman author of the early twentieth century.

Have you experienced the loss of a loved one?
How has that changed you?

Is there a creative community you
can be part of? How will it inspire
you and help your talents grow?

I am I CAN I WILL

Write your own story. Use the details of your life now, and how you got to this place. Then use your imagination to write about the future you want.

"THE LOVE OF GOD WAS SHED ABROAD IN HER HEART, AND IT FOUND EXPRESSION IN ACTS OF BENEVOLENCE TO HIS CHILDREN." —FROM AN 1854 OBITUARY FOR CATHERINE FERGUSON

Catherine "Katy" Ferguson grew up with a deep compassion for poor, motherless children of all races. Born into slavery, she was orphaned at age seven when her enslaver, who was a church elder, sold her mother away. The awful pain of never seeing her mother again must have felt unbearable, yet Katy showed no bitterness or anger toward anyone. She remembered that before her mother was ripped away from her, she laid her hand on Katy's head and gave her to God. This planted a strong religious faith in Katy that shaped her life. Although her enslaver's wife refused to let Katy learn to read, she knew the scriptures by heart. Finally, at age seventeen, Katy's freedom was bought by a woman from her church. Katy repaid the woman by baking and selling cakes. Briefly married at eighteen, Katy bore two children who did not survive. From then on, she devoted her life and love to caring for the children of the streets. She fed, clothed, and mothered them, gave them religious instruction, and opened what many believe was the first Sunday School in New York City. Although Katy gave away all that she earned, the respect from her community and the love of the forty-eight homeless or neglected children she raised were priceless.

I *am* **I** CAN **I** _WILL_

Write about a time when you felt like you
couldn't overcome the challenges in front
of you. How did you react? And how did you
eventually find a way to move forward?

Have you ever done something kind for
someone without expecting anything in return?
How did it make you feel?

130

What gives you faith? Is it religion? A friend or family member? Your own determination?

VERNICE "FLYGIRL" ARMOUR (B. 1973)
I WILL ACHIEVE THE UNEXPECTED.

"WHATEVER YOU DO, DON'T BE AVERAGE."
—VERNICE ARMOUR

It came as little surprise to Vernice Armour's friends and family when she announced that she was going to join the military. After all, it was in her blood. Her grandfather, father, and stepfather were all decorated military officers. These role models instilled in her the importance of serving others, and of being a strong leader who guides those less fortunate. While she had a supportive family who gave her opportunities to grow and learn, in the bigger world she saw that women, especially African American women, did not always have equal opportunities. Determined to open the door for herself and others, Vernice first pursued her own childhood dream to be a mounted police officer. Taking a year off from college, she became the first African American woman on the Nashville, Tennessee, motorcycle squad. Volunteering for tough shifts and standing strong in challenging situations, she earned the respect of her fellow officers and the community. Soon she headed for the Marines, where there had never been an African American woman aviator. Vernice was determined to change that. Graduating number one among more than two hundred Marine pilot trainees, she flew Cobra helicopters in the Iraq War, testing her limits and becoming the first Black combat pilot in all the armed forces. Today, as a motivational speaker, consultant, and author, she is committed to helping others see their potential to go beyond average and take flight as well.

What does it mean to open doors
for someone? In what ways can
you do that in your family, school,
or community? Or even for yourself?

_____
_____
_____
_____
_____
_____
_____
_____

Do you have an interest, hobby,
or goal that some might consider
"uncommon" or "impossible" for a girl or
for a Black person? How can you handle
these attitudes and stay true to yourself?

_____
_____
_____
_____
_____
_____
_____
_____

Name one role model who has set an example
for you. How have their accomplishments
helped you see your own potential?

QUEEN TIYE (CA. 1400–1340 BCE)

I WILL BRIDGE DIFFERENCES AND UNITE.

"... KEEP ON SENDING JOY BETWEEN OUR KINGDOMS."
—KING TUSHRATTA OF MITANNI TO
QUEEN TIYE OF EGYPT

Although she was married to Pharaoh Amenhotep III of Egypt, and grandmother to King Tutankhamen, Queen Tiye did not take a backseat to anyone. She had been raised in the nearby nation of Nubia, where it was customary for women to be trained as leaders. Tiye was smart, wise, and ambitious. But instead of competing with Amenhotep, she used the qualities she'd learned to lead quietly behind the scenes, ensuring peace and harmony inside and outside the palace. She acted as an ambassador to other nations, traveling to negotiate difficult situations with their rulers. Sometimes she helped open new trade routes. Sometimes she stopped highwaymen from attacking Egyptian merchants as they passed through foreign lands. Sometimes she even helped prevent wars. Some people would have avoided such a big responsibility, worried that they couldn't follow through. But Tiye was committed to doing her best for her people. She was also known for making good on her promises. By being trustworthy and perfecting the art of compromise, she ensured her people's future and her own. Doors opened around the world. Gradually her role grew into something much like today's US secretary of state, and she was second in charge to the pharaoh. Tiye was also a calming influence for her family and household during difficult times. When Amenhotep III died and their son became pharaoh, Tiye's wisdom and international goodwill was reassuring and helped to keep Egypt a nation of peace and prosperity. Ancient art depicts her as a uniter of people, and her image of benevolence endures today.

How can being committed to helping
someone else help you to grow? Think
of someone you helped and how you became
a better person from the experience.

What does it mean to you to be trustworthy? How do you show others that you are trustworthy?

PHILLIS WHEATLEY (CA. 1753–1784)

I WILL LIVE WITH HOPE.

"O MY SOUL, SINK NOT INTO DESPAIR, VIRTUE IS NEAR THEE, AND WITH GENTLE HAND WOULD NOW EMBRACE THEE . . ." —PHILLIS WHEATLEY

Phillis Wheatley was brought to America when she was seven or eight years old. Seized from Senegal or Gambia in West Africa, she was wrapped in a dirty carpet, crammed into the hold of a ship, and sent across the sea to be enslaved. Delivered around 1761 to Boston, Massachusetts, she was cold, starving, and alone. Fearing what other terrors awaited her, Phillis had every reason to feel hopeless . . . until she found her voice. The tiny, frail girl was purchased by the Wheatley family, and, like other enslaved workers, she was forbidden to read and write. But the Wheatley children recognized her intelligence, and soon Phillis was racing through the Bible and Greek and Latin classics. She was writing, too, modeling her words after the tone and rhythms of the books she read. By age twelve, Phillis was writing exquisite poetry that intertwined her thoughts with current issues of faith and politics. Writing brought healing and hope for a better life. At age eighteen, with the help of Mrs. Wheatley, Phillis published a book of poems that became internationally acclaimed, and General George Washington invited her to read for him. She became America's first celebrated and published Black female poet. When Phillis died in her thirties, she was still writing and hoping to publish again. But her art lived on, and more works are still being discovered. Today her name appears on community centers across the country because they, like Phillis, nourish hope.

How do you use your creative
talents to express yourself?

How does Phillis's unusual success
help you think in a bigger way
about your own opportunities?

Write a poem about your own life
and your dreams. It can be any
format—rhyme, free-form, or haiku.

joy freedom hope
peace victory

"YOU HAVE TO UNDERSTAND THAT YOUR WORK WILL HAVE TO BE MIGHTY SO THAT IT CAN DO YOUR SPEAKING." — KIZZMEKIA "KIZZY" CORBETT

You may not have heard the name Kizzmekia "Kizzy" Corbett before, but her work has changed people's lives. Kizzy is one of the scientists who helped develop a successful vaccine for the COVID-19 coronavirus. And she believes that people of color need to be recognized for their accomplishments—especially one who protects the world's health and safety. Growing up in a small North Carolina community, working hard to succeed was a family value—especially when success meant helping other people. Drawn to math and science, Kizzy worked hard to pursue a career in medicine. With a PhD in microbiology and immunology, Kizzy had already been developing coronavirus vaccines at the National Institutes of Health (NIH) when COVID-19 began spreading in early 2020. She and her NIH team quickly began working with the drug company Moderna to find a safe and effective vaccine for this deadly new virus. At just thirty-four years old, she was leading a team of much more experienced scientists as they raced against time to literally save the world. When the president of the United States visited NIH in late 2020 to learn about the vaccine, Kizzy stood tall and proud as lead scientist, and she let her mighty work speak for itself. People might have doubted this young Black woman, but no one could deny her successful results. She could finally share with the world that lives were about to be saved. Kizzy continues to use social media, television, and even visits to neighborhoods to encourage others to trust her work and get this life-saving vaccine.

What work have you done that proudly speaks for itself? A school assignment, a great story, or a piece of art? How does it feel to claim this as *your* work?

Have you ever thought about working in a science, technology, engineering, or math field? Does knowing that not many Black women are doing this inspire you to try?

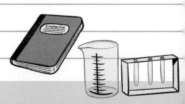

When you're under pressure to finish an important piece of work, it's easy to feel overwhelmed. How do you overcome this feeling? Write down steps you can take to help you stay focused and meet your goal.

TONI MORRISON (1931–2019)
I WILL DO WHAT NEEDS TO BE DONE.

> ## "IF THERE'S A BOOK THAT YOU WANT TO READ, BUT IT HASN'T BEEN WRITTEN YET, THEN YOU MUST WRITE IT."
> ### —TONI MORRISON

This simple piece of advice from Chloe Anthony Wofford Morrison, better known as bestselling author Toni Morrison, guided her and the many students and writers she mentored. Growing up in a small Ohio town in the 1930s and '40s, Toni simply could not find the books she wanted to read—stories about Black people from all eras and experiences, interacting with one another within our own communities. Stories about us, for us. Eventually she knew that she would have to write them herself. Toni's family had always loved telling traditional African American tales and ghost stories and singing songs, and she had listened with all her heart. They sparked her imagination and defined her deepest self, and they stayed with her as she studied drama and American literature in college. She took a job as the first Black female fiction editor with the world's largest publisher, Random House, and excelled at editing other people's work. But she still could not find stories that spoke to her. So she began getting up every day at 4:00 a.m. to write her own stories, in a slow and familiar rhythm, as if entertaining her family around their dinner table. She pulled from events in her tiny hometown and the men and women she knew. Soon Random House was publishing *her* books, and millions of people read them. Filling what she called a wide vacuum in Black literature, her work has been praised globally and received literature's highest honors. Always humble, Toni remained dedicated to telling the stories she had to tell.

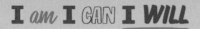

If something you want doesn't exist, invent it.
A book, a movie, a new cookie flavor, or a
board game—make a list of your new ideas.
How will you make them happen?

What stories do you want to tell? What people or events in your life do you want to turn into stories to share with the world? Spark your own storytelling imagination by writing a few sentences describing a character or story line that draws from your own experiences.

MARIAN ANDERSON (1897–1993)

I WILL SOAR IN BEAUTY AND POSITIVITY.

> "AS LONG AS YOU KEEP A PERSON DOWN, SOME PART OF YOU HAS TO BE DOWN THERE TO HOLD HIM DOWN, SO IT MEANS YOU CANNOT SOAR AS YOU OTHERWISE MIGHT." —MARIAN ANDERSON

Renowned African American opera singer Marian Anderson enjoyed magnificent success in Europe. Her fans included famed Italian conductor Arturo Toscanini, who said that a voice like Marian's is heard only once in a hundred years. But even after her triumphant return to America in 1935, she still faced the same racial prejudice that had driven her away five years before. When the segregated Constitution Hall, owned by the Daughters of the American Revolution (DAR), refused to host her 1939 performance, she was devastated. But this was one of many such insults throughout her long career, and Marian refused to allow these incidents to break her spirit. She became known for maintaining her dignity in the face of bigotry. Simply bewildered and saddened by the DAR incident, she couldn't understand why people would want to stop her from doing such a beautiful thing as singing. First Lady Eleanor Roosevelt and many other prominent DAR members immediately resigned in protest, and Marian was offered a much larger stage—the National Mall in Washington, DC. Denied the audience in the DAR's small concert hall, Marian Anderson's voice soared to reach millions when her Easter Sunday concert was broadcast around the world. She gained enormous international recognition for her outstanding talent and later became the first African American member of the prestigious New York Metropolitan Opera.

When challenging things happen to you, what actions do you take to stay positive?

_____
_____
_____
_____
_____
_____
_____
_____

What we say or do to others also affects how we feel. Fill in the blanks: When I smile it makes me feel _____. When I frown or scowl it makes me feel _____.

_____
_____
_____
_____
_____
_____
_____

Have you ever tried to keep someone down?
Write honestly about what happened. How did
it make you feel? How did it change you?

CHEER

COMFORT UNDERSTAND MOTIVATE

ENCOURAGE

INSPIRE PRAISE UPLIFT

SUPPORT

"LIFE IS NOT A DRESS REHEARSAL. SO I HAVE TRIED TO FOCUS ON MAKING LIFE MEANINGFUL."
—BARBARA HILLARY

Don't ever believe that you're too old or too young to follow your dreams. Barbara Hillary didn't. At the age of seventy-five, she became one of the oldest people, and the first Black woman, to stand on the North Pole. She told people that she was screaming, jumping up and down, and had never experienced such sheer joy and excitement. Four years later she made another epic trek to the South Pole. Nothing stopped her. Not age, not having to learn to ski, not even her difficulty breathing from surviving two rounds of cancer. It's a long way to the ends of the Earth from the poor neighborhood in New York City where Barbara grew up. But she was a reader and a dreamer and a doer. She fell in love with stories of extreme adventure, such as *Robinson Crusoe*, and imagined traveling to places where others didn't go. And she prepared. Perhaps some part of her knew that she was destined to push beyond the supposed limitations of "old" age. In college she studied the science of aging, called gerontology, and learned never to put an age limit on herself. After a successful career in nursing, when most people her age were retiring, she was just getting started on her new path as an adventurer. Following a serious physical and mental training regimen, she not only conquered the Poles, but she dog-sledded in Quebec, photographed polar bears in Manitoba, and lived with nomads in Mongolia the year before she died—at the ripe young age of eighty-eight.

Are you living the life you want to live? What can you do today, or prepare to do later, that will fill you with joy or satisfaction or pride?

Can you think of a person who inspires you with the way they live with energy and purpose? What do you admire the most about them?

"I LOVE SEEING PEOPLE BE SUCCESSFUL! I LOVE THAT. IT'S WONDERFUL. THERE'S ENOUGH ROOM FOR EVERYBODY. THE MESSAGE I LIKE TO CONVEY TO WOMEN AND GIRLS ACROSS THE GLOBE IS THAT THERE IS NO GLASS CEILING." —VENUS WILLIAMS

Venus Williams became a professional women's tennis player at the age of fourteen. Called a child prodigy, the 6' 1" teenager played with more power and speed than any women's tennis player the world had ever seen. In the coming years she would learn both the physical and emotional demands of playing tennis at the highest level. Venus continued to improve her game, and in 2000 she won Wimbledon, perhaps the sport's most famous tournament; the US Open; and two Olympic gold medals. This was just the beginning of a long career, during which she would achieve groundbreaking success as well as suffer devastating setbacks, including being replaced at the top by her younger sister, Serena. For Venus, this was simply another challenge, another chance to work her way back up, and a realization that sharing the spotlight didn't diminish her glow. Venus Williams has played professional tennis long past the age when most players retire. She wins less often than she used to, and her sister has become the more famous and celebrated player. But that's okay with Venus. She remains steady and determined, and you can never count her out. She's also an entrepreneur and the founder of two thriving design companies. Whether in tennis or in business, Venus is proof that there's enough success for all to share.

Have you ever experienced jealousy when someone else received praise or accomplished something you were also trying to achieve? How did you handle the situation? Would you handle it differently now?

Praising other people when they do well is not only good "sportsmanship," it also has a positive effect on you. How can you uplift other Black girls, whether it's on the sports field, in the classroom, or in an after-school activity?

GREAT JOB!

Take a moment to think about the women you've met, and write what you've learned about yourself on this journey so far. Fill in the spaces below when you're ready. You can come back to this page to review your statements or to fill them in at any time.

Declarations for Myself

I WILL:

I WILL:

I WILL:

I WILL:

I WILL:

Write about a special woman in your life who guides you, inspires you, and in whose footsteps you walk. Draw her picture and write about her below. What is a quote that defines her?

HER NAME:

HER PICTURE:

HER QUOTE:

HER STORY:

Although you have reached the end of this journal, your journey to self-discovery and self-direction is a continuing process. Think about where you are right now and, when you're ready, complete these empowering statements for yourself.

I AM:

I CAN:

I WILL:

SOURCES

These are only a few of the books, articles, and websites that will give you a deeper look into the lives of the women you've just met. We invite you to look even further, to new sources, to discover more about these heroines and many others beyond this book!

—Ruth and Cynthia

BOOKS

Armour, Vernice. *Zero to Breakthrough: The 7-Step, Battle-Tested Method for Accomplishing Goals That Matter.* New York: Avery, 2011.

Gale-Cengage, eds. *Contemporary Black Biography: Profiles from the International Black Community.* Vol. 22. Boston: Gale-Cengage Learning, 2009.

Harrison, Vashti. *Little Leaders: Bold Women in Black History.* New York: Little, Brown Books for Young Readers, 2017.

Hudson, Cheryl Willis. *Brave. Black. First.: 50+ African American Women Who Changed the World.* New York: Crown Books for Young Readers, 2020.

Jacobs Carter, Cynthia. *Africana Woman: Her Story Through Time.* Washington, DC: National Geographic, 2003.

Jacobs Carter, Cynthia, ed. *Freedom In My Heart: Voices from the United States National Slavery Museum.* Washington, DC: National Geographic, 2008.

Pellum, Kimberly Brown. *Black Women in Science: A Black History Book for Kids.* New York: Rockridge Press, 2019.

Pinkney, Andrea Davis. *Let It Shine: Stories of Black Women Freedom Fighters.* New York: Clarion Books, 2013.

ARTICLES/MEDIA

Brown, Brené. "The Wisdom of Viola Davis: 'Anger is Underrated.'" *Hollywood Reporter*, vol. 424, no. 40. Dec. 5, 2018.

Chiang, Mona. "Out of this world: soar into space with a history-making astronaut." *Science World*, vol. 63, no. 5–6, Nov. 13, 2006.

Goodyear, Dana. "Kamala Harris Makes Her Case." *The New Yorker*. July 15, 2019. https://www.newyorker.com/magazine/2019/07/22/kamala-harris-makes-her-case.

Huber, Eliza. "People with Disabilities Deserve Great Style—& I've Made it My Life's Work." *Refinery 29*. July 24, 2020. https://www.refinery29.com/en-us/2020/07/9901574/adaptive-clothing-fashion-stephanie-thomas-cur8able.

Mark, Joshua J. "Tiye." *World History Encyclopedia*. July 18, 2011. https://www.worldhistory.org/tiye/.

Subbaraman, Nidhi. "This COVID-vaccine designer is tackling vaccine hesitancy—in churches and on Twitter." *Nature*. February 11, 2021. https://www.nature.com/articles/d41586-021-00338-y.

Wilson, Elizabeth B. "The Queen Who Would be King." *Smithsonian Magazine*. September 2006. https://www.smithsonianmag.com /history/the-queen-who-would-be-king-130328511/.

COLLECTIONS: WEBSITES AND DATABASES

Biography, various pages. https://biography.com.

Encyclopedia Britannica Biographies, various pages. *Encyclopedia Britannica*. https://www.britannica.com/biographies.

Gale. "US History: African American History" https://www.gale .com/african-american-history.

Gale in Context: Biography, various pages. Gale. https://www.gale .com/c/in-context-biography.

She Made History: Her Story: Trailblazers, Barrier Breakers, Leaders, various pages. http://shemadehistory.com/.

World History Encyclopedia, various pages. https://www.worldhistory.org.

ABOUT THE AUTHORS

Dr. Cynthia Jacobs Carter works in philanthropy at the Smithsonian Institution's National Museum of African American History and Culture. She is the author of the National Geographic books *Africana Woman: Her Story Through Time* and *Freedom in My Heart: Voices from the National Slavery Museum*, which was nominated by the NAACP Image Awards for Best Literary Work. Cynthia's gift for storytelling brings alive the Black female experience for women of all ages. Having six granddaughters helps inspire her to celebrate young women. Holding a doctorate in educational leadership and a master's degree in international education from George Washington University, Cynthia has connected especially with young women as an instructor and lecturer in Africana women's studies at GW and Georgetown Universities. While working in philanthropy at Howard University, she was curator for the exhibition "Women of the African Diaspora," which toured the White House, the World Bank, and George Washington and Georgetown Universities. Cynthia serves with several local and national organizations and their boards, including The Links, Incorporated. As a development officer she has grown philanthropic programs at Africare, the Smithsonian Center for Folklife and Cultural Heritage, and at the National Museum of African American History and Culture, where she founded the Harriet Tubman Legacy Society.

Ruth Chamblee is a publishing and marketing professional who leads the Content Marketing Strategy & Promotion team for National Geographic Kids Books. Her early career included brand management marketing at Richardson-Vicks, a division of Procter and Gamble, and membership marketing for the Smithsonian Institution Books and Recordings divisions. For more than three decades she has designed and carried out multifaceted strategic marketing initiatives for countless National Geographic books, and her guidance has helped bring new voices to fill key niches in the children's book market. She is a board member of the Children's Book Council and Chairman of the Board for Every Child a Reader. Her vision for *I Am, I Can, I Will* arose from her realization that knowing and honoring our ancestors can contribute to self-awareness, self-empowerment, and self-love for her, her daughter, and all little Black girls.

ABOUT THE ILLUSTRATOR

Steffi Walthall is a US illustrator and storyteller based in Virginia. Steffi's work is rooted in human-centric stories that celebrate diversity and the unending endurance of the human spirit. She has worked on a number of titles with publishers such as Scholastic, Simon & Schuster, Penguin Random House, and Macmillan. Her work can also be found in magazines and newspapers like *The New York Times*, *The New Yorker*, and *Bloomberg*. When she isn't working on a new project, Steffi can be found taking photos on her 35-mm film camera, watching horror movies, and playing *a lot* of video games.